PRINCEWILL LAGANG

Lifelong Partnership: Aging Gracefully as a Couple

Contents

1

Introduction

As the sun sets on the horizon of life, the journey of aging takes on a new dimension when experienced in the company of a lifelong partner. This book delves into the theme of aging as a couple, exploring the profound significance of companionship and partnership that spans the test of time. The chapters ahead will unravel the intricacies of growing old together, offering insights into the dynamics that emerge as two individuals navigate the uncharted waters of later life side by side.

The journey of aging together is a testament to the enduring power of love and commitment. It is a journey that begins in the fervor of youth, where promises are exchanged amidst dreams and aspirations. As time weaves its tapestry, the bond between partners deepens, creating a reservoir of shared experiences, memories, and emotions that only the passage of years can bestow.

This book seeks to explore the multidimensional aspects of aging together - from the physical changes that accompany the golden years, to the emotional nuances that are unique to partners who have weathered the storms of life collectively. As wrinkles mark the passage of time on weathered skin, they also mirror the stories etched in the heart.

The complexities of aging are not solely a matter of individual experience; they extend to the shared journey of a couple. The chapters that follow will delve into the challenges that may arise, as well as the triumphs that result from navigating the terrain of aging hand in hand. From facing health concerns to adapting to the evolving roles within the relationship, the aging process ushers in transformations that demand unwavering support and understanding.

Through personal anecdotes, expert insights, and intimate reflections, this book will guide you through the joys and sorrows, the laughter and tears, and the growth and renewal that aging as a couple can bring. Each chapter will shed light on a different facet of this journey, ultimately painting a comprehensive portrait of the unique dynamics that emerge when two individuals commit to growing old together.

So, embark on this exploration of aging as a couple, where the passage of time is not a solitary endeavor, but rather a shared odyssey that binds hearts and souls in a way that only a lifelong partnership can. As the pages unfold, may you find resonance, inspiration, and a deeper appreciation for the intricate dance of aging gracefully side by side.

2

Embracing Aging as a Team

I n the intricate tapestry of life, the threads of aging are woven into the very fabric of a couple's journey. As the years advance, the concept of aging transcends the boundaries of individual experience, transforming into a shared endeavor that requires collaboration, understanding, and resilience. In this chapter, we delve into the profound essence of aging as a team, where partners unite their strengths to navigate the challenges and joys of growing old together.

The journey of aging is often associated with physical changes, health concerns, and evolving roles. Yet, when faced together, these challenges can be approached with a sense of mutual support that bolsters the spirit. Just as a well-matched team can achieve remarkable feats, a couple that confronts the trials of aging as a united front can harness their collective wisdom and fortitude to overcome obstacles that might seem insurmountable alone.

Mutual support becomes the cornerstone of aging as a team. The understanding that one's partner is navigating similar territory creates a unique bond, fostering empathy and compassion. When one faces health issues, the other stands as a pillar of strength, providing not only physical assistance but also emotional solace. The act of caring becomes a reciprocal exchange, emphasizing the essence of partnership in its truest form.

Moreover, aging as a team calls for a reimagining of roles and responsibilities within the relationship. As careers transition, children grow and leave the nest, and hobbies may shift, partners find themselves in a delicate dance of adapting to new routines and redefining their identities. The ability to communicate openly and explore these changes together can lead to a newfound sense of purpose and fulfillment, fostering a deeper connection between individuals who have journeyed through life hand in hand.

This chapter will explore the various ways in which partners can provide mutual support, celebrate each other's achievements, and offer solace during moments of vulnerability. Through anecdotes and expert insights, it will illuminate the strength that emerges when couples view aging not as an isolated experience, but as a collaborative effort. The examples shared within these pages will serve as a testament to the power of unity in the face of adversity and the beauty of shared laughter in the presence of life's uncertainties.

In embracing aging as a team, couples can discover that the journey becomes not merely a succession of years but a testament to the enduring power of love and companionship. The chapters that follow will continue to explore the nuances of this journey, unveiling the layers of meaning and depth that emerge when two souls intertwine in the dance of growing old together.

3

Communication Across the Years

As time weaves its intricate tapestry, communication between partners evolves, transforming into a dynamic reflection of the shared journey. The ability to connect through conversation takes on a new dimension as the years advance, highlighting the importance of adaptability and understanding in maintaining meaningful interactions. In this chapter, we delve into the ever-changing landscape of communication across the years and the significance of fostering connections that endure the test of time.

Communication, often described as the lifeblood of relationships, undergoes a subtle transformation as partners age together. What once was a whirlwind of shared dreams and animated discussions may evolve into quieter moments of companionship, where words become vehicles for shared comfort and understanding. The silences between sentences can hold as much significance as the words themselves, as partners learn to communicate not only through speech but also through gestures, glances, and the unspoken language of familiarity.

Embracing the evolving nature of communication is essential for nurturing the connection that binds partners together. The topics of conversation shift to encompass the experiences and memories accumulated over the years, intertwining past, present, and future. Reflecting on shared adventures, celebrating milestones, and reminiscing about cherished moments become threads that connect partners across the tapestry of time.

Adaptability emerges as a cornerstone in maintaining meaningful conversations as partners age. As physical capabilities and interests change, the ability to adapt one's communication style becomes paramount. Patience and active listening become tools that facilitate understanding, allowing partners to bridge potential gaps in comprehension or to address the slower pace that might accompany the passage of years.

In this chapter, we will explore strategies for nurturing effective communication across the years. We will delve into the art of listening with empathy, the power of validating each other's perspectives, and the ways in which partners can encourage open dialogue even in the face of differing opinions. Through real-life stories and expert advice, we will uncover the techniques that help partners maintain a sense of connection and intimacy as they navigate the nuanced landscape of aging together.

In the backdrop of life's complexities, communication serves as the thread that weaves hearts together, anchoring partners in the shared story they continue to write. The subsequent chapters will continue to illuminate the multifaceted aspects of aging as a couple, delving deeper into the layers of emotion, growth, and transformation that unfold when two individuals communicate across the years, their voices harmonizing like a melody that resonates through time.

4

Navigating Health Changes

Aging brings with it a journey of transformation, not only in the external landscape but also within the very fabric of our being. Physical and mental health changes become integral chapters in this story, and as partners age together, these changes ripple through their shared existence. In this chapter, we delve into the profound impact of health changes on relationships, exploring the resilience required to navigate these challenges while remaining connected in mind, body, and spirit.

The intertwined nature of partnership means that when one partner experiences a shift in health, the other is also inevitably affected. Physical ailments, whether minor or significant, can reshape daily routines and the ways in which partners interact. The ability to adapt and provide support in the face of these changes becomes a testament to the enduring strength of the relationship.

Equally impactful are the shifts in mental and emotional well-being that may arise as partners age. Mood fluctuations, cognitive changes, and the emotional toll of life's challenges can strain even the most resilient bonds. As caregivers or sources of solace, partners play a crucial role in each other's mental health journey, emphasizing the importance of empathy and understanding during times of vulnerability.

Coping with health changes while remaining connected necessitates a delicate balance of self-care and mutual support. It requires a willingness to communicate openly about challenges, fears, and needs, while also allowing space for personal growth and adaptation. In this chapter, we will delve into strategies that foster understanding, such as seeking professional guidance when necessary, practicing active listening, and fostering an environment of patience and compassion.

Moreover, embracing the concept of "we" over "me" can become a guiding principle as partners navigate health changes together. By viewing challenges as shared experiences, partners can tap into the strength that emerges when two hearts beat in unison, facing adversity with courage and determination.

Through anecdotes, expert insights, and practical advice, this chapter will provide a roadmap for maintaining connection while addressing health challenges. It will showcase the resilience that can blossom when partners stand united, adapting to new circumstances with grace and unwavering support. Ultimately, the path of navigating health changes as a couple reflects the essence of companionship in its purest form—embracing every chapter of life's journey with love, respect, and the commitment to face the unknown hand in hand.

As the journey unfolds, the subsequent chapters will continue to explore the intricate dynamics of aging as a couple, illuminating the ways in which partners can foster a connection that transcends the trials of time and health, emerging stronger and more united than ever before.

5

Cultivating Shared Activities

Amidst the tapestry of aging together, shared activities and interests serve as vibrant threads that bind partners in moments of joy and connection. As time marches on, the significance of these shared pursuits becomes ever more apparent, acting as a bridge that spans the years and fosters a sense of togetherness. In this chapter, we delve into the importance of cultivating shared activities, both as a continuation of familiar passions and as a means of discovering new avenues that align with the evolving needs and abilities of partners.

Shared activities serve as a conduit for partners to explore the world and each other anew. Engaging in hobbies that have been cherished for years can rekindle memories and create a sense of continuity in the face of change. Whether it's gardening, traveling, or dancing, these pursuits infuse life with moments of shared laughter, achievement, and exploration, reminding partners of the vibrant spirit that has carried them through the years.

However, the journey of aging often demands adaptability. Interests and physical capabilities may shift, prompting the need for the discovery of new activities that resonate with the present moment. Partners must remain open to exploring uncharted territories and creating shared experiences that reflect their current reality. A willingness to try new things not only broadens horizons but also fosters a sense of shared growth and curiosity.

In this chapter, we will explore strategies for continuing cherished activities and for embracing the exploration of new ones. We will discuss the importance of communication in identifying interests that align with changing circumstances and the benefits of compromise when partners have differing preferences. Furthermore, we will delve into the value of finding activities that cater to both partners' needs and abilities, ensuring that the journey remains inclusive and enjoyable for both.

Through anecdotes, practical advice, and expert insights, this chapter will illuminate the ways in which shared activities can infuse the journey of aging with vibrancy and connection. Whether it's the thrill of learning a new skill together or the comfort of revisiting familiar pastimes, these shared moments enrich the tapestry of companionship, serving as a testament to the enduring power of partnership across the passage of time.

As the subsequent chapters unfold, the exploration of aging as a couple will continue to unveil the layers of emotion, growth, and transformation that emerge when two individuals commit to nurturing their bond through shared experiences, echoing the sentiment that the heart remains forever young when enlivened by the presence of a kindred spirit.

6

Intimacy and Connection in Later Life

As the years unfold, the flame of intimacy and emotional connection takes on a unique radiance, illuminating the path of couples who have aged together. The chapters of life's journey may evolve, but the essence of romance and the depth of emotional closeness remain steadfast, weaving a tapestry of love that transcends the boundaries of time. In this chapter, we delve into the vital role of intimacy and emotional connection in later life, exploring how couples can navigate the landscape of aging while maintaining a bond that continues to flourish.

Intimacy, in all its forms, serves as a cornerstone of companionship that evolves and deepens with the passage of time. While the physical expressions of intimacy may change, the emotional and spiritual connections that underpin them remain vibrant. Partners find new ways to connect, whether it's through holding hands, sharing affectionate gestures, or embracing the quiet comfort of each other's presence. The ability to communicate desires, needs, and boundaries becomes crucial in navigating this evolving terrain.

Emotional closeness, too, takes on a profound significance as couples age. Partners become each other's confidants, offering a safe haven for vulnerability and the assurance of unwavering support. Conversations deepen, delving into the realms of past memories, dreams, and reflections on the journey they've shared. The foundation of trust that has been built over the years enables partners to explore the depths of their emotional landscapes without fear.

Maintaining a fulfilling romantic bond and emotional connection requires intentional effort and a willingness to adapt to the changing landscape of desire and need. This chapter will delve into the strategies that can enrich the intimate aspects of a relationship, including open communication about desires and preferences, the importance of prioritizing quality time together, and the value of continuous exploration of each other's emotional worlds.

Through real-life stories, expert insights, and practical advice, this chapter will shed light on the myriad ways in which intimacy and emotional closeness can be cultivated and sustained. Whether through shared laughter, gentle touch, or the vulnerability of authentic conversations, these expressions of connection serve as a testament to the enduring power of love in the face of life's challenges and joys.

As the journey continues, the subsequent chapters will continue to explore the nuances of aging as a couple, offering insights into the layers of emotion, growth, and transformation that emerge when two individuals nurture their bond through intimacy, communication, and unwavering devotion, a beacon of love that remains aglow amidst the tapestry of time.

7

Building a Supportive Social Circle

In the symphony of life, friendships and social connections are the harmonious notes that enrich the melody of companionship. As partners journey through the seasons of aging, the significance of maintaining a vibrant social circle becomes all the more apparent. The tapestry of life is woven not only with the threads of partnership but also with the threads of community, creating a network of support that offers solace, joy, and shared experiences. In this chapter, we delve into the importance of building a supportive social circle and provide insights into how couples can stay socially engaged, fostering a strong sense of community as they navigate the journey of aging together.

Friendships and social connections serve as vital components of a fulfilling life, offering opportunities for shared laughter, empathetic conversations, and the exchange of wisdom. As partners age, the bonds formed with friends over the years become pillars of strength, providing an external source of support that complements the intimate connection shared within the relationship. These connections act as mirrors, reflecting the essence of the journey and offering perspectives that enrich the tapestry of life.

Staying socially engaged requires intention and effort, especially as the years advance and circumstances change. Partners can explore activities that align with their interests and passions, seeking out clubs, groups, or organizations that resonate with their values. Engaging in volunteer work, joining community events, or participating in workshops can serve as avenues for meeting new people and nurturing relationships that contribute to a sense of belonging.

Cultivating a supportive social circle also involves maintaining existing friendships and forming new connections. Regular interactions, whether in person or through digital means, can help partners stay connected with friends from different phases of life. Additionally, the act of making new friends requires an open heart and a willingness to embrace diverse perspectives, enriching the fabric of the couple's social tapestry.

In this chapter, we will explore strategies for building and nurturing a supportive social circle. We will discuss the importance of effective communication and active listening in maintaining friendships, as well as the benefits of seeking out opportunities for shared activities that resonate with both partners. Moreover, we will delve into the significance of celebrating milestones and creating memories with friends, enriching the journey with shared experiences that contribute to a sense of belonging.

Through anecdotes, expert insights, and practical advice, this chapter will illuminate the ways in which couples can weave a network of social connections that uplift and enrich their lives. These connections serve as a testament to the power of community in the journey of aging, reinforcing the idea that the heart expands to accommodate not only the love shared between partners but also the bonds formed with kindred spirits along the way.

As the subsequent chapters unfold, the exploration of aging as a couple will continue to unveil the layers of emotion, growth, and transformation that emerge when two individuals foster connections that transcend the boundaries of their relationship, creating a symphony of support and camaraderie that echoes through the passage of time.

8

Reflecting on Legacy and Life's Journey

As partners traverse the tapestry of life, there comes a time when reflections on the journey become a precious gift to each other. The process of looking back on life experiences, cherishing memories, and contemplating the legacy one leaves behind becomes a poignant exploration that deepens the bond between partners. In this chapter, we delve into the transformative power of reflecting on life's journey, discussing how sharing memories, stories, and wisdom can enrich the connection between couples who have aged together.

The act of reflecting on life's journey is an opportunity for partners to gather the scattered fragments of memories and weave them into a tapestry of shared history. It's a chance to revisit milestones, reminisce about adventures, and celebrate triumphs that have shaped the course of their lives. As partners exchange stories and reflect on their experiences, they gain a deeper understanding of the intricate threads that have woven their paths together.

The process of reflecting on legacy extends beyond the tangible aspects of life. It's an exploration of the values, beliefs, and life lessons that have guided each partner's choices. Contemplating the impact one has made on the world and the people around them creates an intimate dialogue between partners, fostering a sense of purpose and fulfillment that echoes through the years.

Sharing memories and stories is an act of vulnerability, as partners open their hearts to reveal the essence of their pasts. This vulnerability fosters a deep sense of connection and empathy, enabling partners to understand each other on a profound level. As stories are exchanged, the wisdom of a life lived fully becomes a treasure trove that both partners can draw from in times of need and inspiration.

In this chapter, we will explore strategies for embracing the process of reflection and sharing life experiences. We will discuss the importance of creating opportunities for open conversations, whether through journaling, storytelling, or reflective activities. Additionally, we will delve into the ways in which partners can create a legacy that reflects their values and passions, ensuring that the impact of their journey ripples through generations to come.

Through real-life stories, expert insights, and practical advice, this chapter will illuminate the ways in which reflecting on life's journey can strengthen the bond between partners who have aged together. These reflections become a treasure trove of shared experiences, a source of comfort in challenging times, and a testament to the enduring power of love and companionship.

As the journey continues, the subsequent chapters will continue to explore the multifaceted aspects of aging as a couple, unraveling the layers of emotion, growth, and transformation that emerge when two individuals embrace the act of reflecting on life's journey, leaving behind footprints of love and wisdom as they continue to write their story together.

9

Coping with Loss and Transition

In the intricate tapestry of aging, the threads of loss and transition are woven alongside the threads of joy and connection. As partners navigate the later years of life, they may inevitably face the challenges of saying goodbye to loved ones and adapting to life's transitions. In this chapter, we delve into the profound journey of coping with loss and navigating change, discussing how couples can provide unwavering support for each other through grief and the shifting landscapes of life.

Loss, whether it be the passing of a loved one or the transition from one life stage to another, can cast a shadow over the journey of aging. Partners who have faced the passage of time together often find themselves confronted with the reality of mortality. The support system built between partners over the years becomes a cornerstone in navigating these difficult moments. The ability to provide solace, empathy, and companionship in times of grief becomes a testament to the strength of the bond.

Coping with loss also demands a deep understanding of the grieving process. Partners may experience grief differently, and the ability to navigate these emotions with compassion and patience is paramount. Effective communication serves as a bridge, allowing partners to share their feelings, fears, and memories openly. Grief can also offer opportunities for reflection on the life shared, honoring the memories of loved ones while finding solace in each other's presence.

Life's transitions, whether it's retirement, downsizing, or changes in health, can also pose challenges that require support and understanding. Partners must adapt to new routines and roles, embracing flexibility and patience as they navigate uncharted territories. Open communication is essential in discussing feelings of uncertainty, sharing aspirations, and jointly planning for the future.

In this chapter, we will explore strategies for supporting each other through loss and life transitions. We will discuss the importance of validating each other's feelings, creating space for shared grief, and seeking external support when needed. Additionally, we will delve into the significance of adapting to new circumstances together, fostering resilience and a sense of unity as partners face change as a team.

Through anecdotes, expert insights, and practical advice, this chapter will illuminate the ways in which partners can navigate the complexities of loss and life transitions while maintaining a connection that endures. These moments of challenge become opportunities for growth, allowing partners to deepen their bond and reaffirm their commitment to being there for each other through every chapter of life.

As the journey unfolds, the subsequent chapters will continue to explore the intricate dynamics of aging as a couple, delving into the layers of emotion, growth, and transformation that emerge when two individuals offer unwavering support and understanding as they navigate the inevitable challenges of loss and transition, a testament to the resilience of love in the face of life's uncertainties.

10

Redefining Retirement Together

The transition to retirement marks a new chapter in the journey of aging, where partners have the opportunity to redefine their lives and relationships. As the rhythms of work and career recede, the canvas of time opens up, offering the chance to shape the future in ways that align with shared aspirations and dreams. In this chapter, we delve into the process of redefining retirement together, exploring the impact of this significant life transition on the relationship and sharing insights into how couples can create fulfilling retirement plans that reflect their joint goals.

The transition to retirement is a juncture that can be met with mixed emotions. While the newfound freedom is invigorating, it can also bring uncertainties and adjustments. Partners may find themselves navigating the landscape of leisure, hobbies, and social engagements with a fresh perspective. Open communication becomes crucial as couples discuss their expectations, desires, and visions for this phase of life. This dialogue allows for the creation of a retirement plan that resonates with both partners, balancing individual interests with shared experiences.

Retirement offers the space to explore new passions, engage in hobbies, and embark on shared adventures that may have been postponed during the busyness of career life. Partners can find fulfillment in activities that resonate with their values and desires, while also nurturing a sense of connection through shared experiences. Whether it's traveling, pursuing creative endeavors, or engaging in philanthropic efforts, these activities contribute to a sense of purpose and joy.

Creating a fulfilling retirement plan involves aligning individual goals with shared aspirations. This requires a willingness to compromise and a spirit of collaboration, as well as a celebration of each partner's uniqueness. Embracing flexibility and adaptability in this new phase of life enables partners to navigate potential challenges and adjustments with grace.

In this chapter, we will explore strategies for navigating the transition to retirement and crafting retirement plans that enrich the couple's journey. We will discuss the value of setting realistic expectations, managing financial considerations, and fostering open conversations about dreams and desires. Furthermore, we will delve into the significance of maintaining a healthy balance between individual pursuits and shared activities, fostering a connection that continues to evolve in the context of retirement.

Through anecdotes, expert insights, and practical advice, this chapter will shed light on the ways in which couples can navigate the complexities of retirement, finding harmony in the pursuit of new adventures and shared goals. The transition to retirement becomes an opportunity for partners to rediscover each other, forging a path that intertwines individual growth with the strength of their enduring bond.

As the subsequent chapters unfold, the exploration of aging as a couple will continue to unveil the layers of emotion, growth, and transformation that emerge when two individuals embrace the process of redefining retirement together, crafting a chapter of life that reflects their shared aspirations and the unique connection that has carried them through the years.

11

Embracing New Roles and Identity

As partners journey through the passage of time, the roles they inhabit and the identities they carry evolve in intricate ways. The process of aging brings with it not only physical changes but also shifts in priorities, aspirations, and self-perception. In this chapter, we delve into the profound exploration of embracing new roles and identity, discussing how couples can navigate the transition to new phases of life while preserving their individuality and the essence of their relationship.

The evolution of roles and identities is a natural part of life's journey. The roles that partners held in their youth, such as parents or career professionals, may undergo transformation as children grow and careers transition. These shifts can evoke a mix of emotions, including nostalgia for the past and anticipation for the future. Partners must navigate the transition with open communication, allowing each other the space to share their thoughts and feelings about the evolving landscape.

Adapting to new roles and identity requires a balance between honoring the past and embracing the present. As partners step into new phases of life, they must also acknowledge the accomplishments and experiences that have shaped their journey thus far. The ability to find common ground in the present while cherishing the memories of the past fosters a sense of continuity and unity.

Preserving individuality within the context of evolving roles is equally essential. Partners must support each other's growth, aspirations, and pursuits, even as they embrace shared experiences. Maintaining a healthy sense of self contributes to a dynamic and fulfilling relationship, as partners come together as equals while also nurturing their independent passions.

In this chapter, we will explore strategies for embracing new roles and identity, both as individuals and as a couple. We will discuss the value of open communication about aspirations and expectations, as well as the significance of creating a space for personal growth and self-discovery. Furthermore, we will delve into the importance of recognizing the strengths that each partner brings to the relationship and celebrating the ways in which these strengths complement one another.

Through anecdotes, expert insights, and practical advice, this chapter will illuminate the ways in which couples can navigate the complexities of embracing new roles and identity, fostering a sense of unity while nurturing individual growth. The evolution of roles becomes an opportunity for partners to rediscover each other in new and meaningful ways, weaving the tapestry of their shared journey with threads of adaptability, respect, and the enduring bond that has carried them through the years.

As the journey unfolds, the subsequent chapters will continue to explore the intricate dynamics of aging as a couple, delving into the layers of emotion, growth, and transformation that emerge when two individuals navigate the evolution of roles and identity with grace, ensuring that the heart's compass continues to point toward the uncharted territories of the future.

12

Reflecting on the Journey

As the sun sets on the horizon of this book, it's time to reflect on the journey of aging gracefully as a couple—a journey that has been marked by growth, challenges, and an abundance of joys. The chapters have delved into the multifaceted aspects of companionship through the passage of time, from embracing aging as a team to fostering intimacy, navigating transitions, and crafting a legacy of love and wisdom. In this final chapter, we pause to reflect on the lessons learned, the bonds strengthened, and the enduring legacy of a resilient lifelong partnership.

The journey of aging together has revealed the profound significance of unity in the face of life's challenges. Partners who have walked this path have discovered that mutual support and understanding are the cornerstones of resilience. As the threads of time weave intricate patterns, they've weathered storms hand in hand, emerging stronger and more united with each shared experience.

Through the chapters, the importance of communication has emerged as a guiding principle. Whether sharing stories, exploring new activities, or navigating health changes, effective communication has been the bridge that has connected partners on a deeper level. Active listening, empathy, and vulnerability have become the tools that foster connection and understanding, illuminating the path through life's uncertainties.

The journey of aging together has also underscored the beauty of adaptation. Partners have navigated shifting landscapes, adapting roles, and embracing new phases of life with grace and courage. The ability to create a retirement plan, build a supportive social circle, and redefine identity while maintaining individuality has been a testament to the strength of love that endures.

As the final pages of this chapter turn, the resounding theme is the power of connection. Partners who age together share more than years; they share the essence of life's experiences. The memories created, the stories shared, and the wisdom exchanged are the legacy that is woven into the fabric of their bond. These connections reverberate through the years, echoing the sentiment that companionship is a gift that only deepens with time.

In closing, fostering a resilient lifelong partnership requires intention, effort, and a commitment to growth. The journey of aging together is not without its challenges, but it is also filled with moments of laughter, shared dreams, and a love that transcends the boundaries of time. As the story of aging gracefully as a couple comes to an end within these pages, may the echoes of the lessons learned and the shared experiences continue to guide partners on their journey of love, connection, and the enduring power of companionship.

As the years continue to unfold, may the love that has been nurtured through this journey serve as a reminder that, just like a fine wine, the bond between partners grows richer and more cherished with each passing year.

Conclusion: Embracing the Journey of Aging Together

As the final words of this journey are penned, it's a moment to pause, reflect, and embrace the profound essence of aging as a team, navigating the tapestry of life side by side. The chapters have unfolded, revealing the intricate layers of growth, challenges, joys, and the enduring power of companionship. From the early pages to this concluding chapter, the thread that has woven its way through the narrative is the importance of unity, communication, and shared aspirations in the journey of aging gracefully as a couple.

The journey of aging together is a testament to the enduring strength of partnership. It's a dance that requires synchrony, as partners move through the chapters of life with unwavering support and understanding. The challenges that arise are met not as individuals but as a united force, standing together to overcome obstacles, navigate transitions, and celebrate victories.

Central to this journey is the art of communication. The ability to share dreams, express feelings, and navigate life's complexities together is a gift that partners bestow upon each other. Active listening and open dialogue form the foundation of a connection that deepens with each shared conversation, each tender moment, and each laughter-filled memory.

As the years unfold, it's important to approach the journey of aging with a spirit of adventure and shared aspirations. Retirement becomes an opportunity to rediscover passions and embrace new horizons. Reflecting on the journey serves as a reminder of the love and growth that have shaped the bond, creating a legacy that will be cherished for generations.

In a world that often emphasizes youth, the journey of aging together stands as a testament to the beauty of growing old gracefully and with dignity. The lines etched on the faces are a map of the experiences shared, the laughter exchanged, and the love nurtured. It's a journey that beckons partners to lean into the unknown with open hearts and a commitment to stand by each other's side, no matter what the future may hold.

So, as the pages of this book close, may the journey of aging together continue to unfold in the hearts of those who have walked this path and those who are yet to embark upon it. May the lessons learned, the wisdom exchanged, and the love shared illuminate the way forward, reminding us that companionship is a gift that becomes more cherished with time. Embrace the journey, communicate with love, and approach the passage of time as a team, for it's in this unity that the true beauty of aging together is revealed.